THE · LITTLE · POCKET · BOOK · OF

CRYSTAL TIPS & CURES

Let the energy of crystals transform your life

THE · LITTLE · POCKET · BOOK · OF

A crystal gift of health, harmony and happiness

PHILIP PERMUTT

CRYSTAL TIPS & CURES

CICO BOOKS

LONDON NEW YORK

This edition published in 2015 by CICO Books
an imprint of Ryland Peters & Small Ltd
20–21 Jockey's Fields, London WC1R 4BW
341 E 116th St, New York NY 10029
www.rylandpeters.com
First published in 2008

10 9 8 7 6 5

ISBN: 978 1 78249 261 0

Printed in China

Editor Samantha Gray
Designer Claire Legemah
Photography Roy Palmer and Geoff Dann
Illustrator Trina Dalziel

Safety Note

Please note that while the descriptions of the properties of some crystals refer to
healing benefits, they are not intended to replace diagnosis of illness or ailments, or
healing or medicine. Always consult your doctor or other health professional in the
case of illness.

Contents

How to Use This Book 6
What Are Crystals? 8
How Crystals Work 10
Choosing Crystals 12
Cleansing Crystals 14
Placing Crystals at Home or at Work 16
Healing with Crystals 18
Crystals on the Move 20
Meditating with Crystals 22
Elixirs 24
Birthstones 26

Crystals by Color
Red 30
Orange 40
Yellow 50
Green 60
Pink 74
Blue 84
Violet 96
Rainbow 106
Multicolored 116
White and Clear 126
Black and Gray 136
Brown 146

Resources 156
Index of Crystals 157
General Index 158
Acknowledgments 160

How to Use This Book

This gem of a guidebook presents more than 100 different crystals, with at-a-glance tips on their uses and benefits...

In the first part of this book, discover how to choose, cleanse and work with the crystals that appeal to you, and understand how crystals can bring about healing when placed on your body's chakras, or energy points (see pages 18-19). You'll also see how simply placing the right selection of crystals can change the energy in your home and workplace to bring health, happiness, abundance and spiritual connection into your life. In the second part of the book, you will find a profile for each crystal, including its astrological association, ruling planet, element and chakra, plus lots of tips for employing crystals at home or at work to ease emotional ailments or enhance your life in a variety of ways.

You can also use this book for daily affirmation. Open it randomly at any crystal page and see which aspects of the chosen crystal you relate to. Contemplate this as a message for you for that day or, if you have the

Having the nurturing, positive energy of popular, readily available crystals such as rose quartz and amethyst in your home will benefit your pets and plants too.

crystal at home, carry it or wear it, if possible, to start enjoying its benefits straightaway.

Whether this book marks the start of your journey with crystals, or another step on your path, take a bold leap and enjoy the experience of change as it happens.

· Identifying Crystals ·

For easy reference, the crystals are divided by color, with 12 color-coded sections helping you to locate them quickly (there's also an index of crystals at the back of this book; see page 157). However, these color sections can really help whenever you have a crystal you can't identify. We're often given crystals as gifts, inherit them from friends, find crystals on holiday, on the beach or elsewhere in nature, and may have no idea of their names or special benefits – and the only obvious attributes are a crystal's color and shape. Of course, crystals vary incredibly in their texture, shape and color, so you may not find a crystal in this book that matches yours exactly. Hopefully, though, it may act as a useful starting point for identification.

✦ **RED CRYSTALS** (pages 30-39) go from blood-red garnet to red jasper.

✦ **ORANGE CRYSTALS** (pages 40-49) include marmalade calcite and flaming sunstone.

✦ **YELLOW CRYSTALS** (pages 50-59) range from honey-colored citrine to pure gold.

✦ **GREEN CRYSTALS** (pages 60-73) encompass lime-green peridot and emerald.

✦ **PINK CRYSTALS** (pages 74-83) embrace candy-pink kunzite and fuchsia-pink eudialyte.

✦ **BLUE CRYSTALS** (pages 84-95) bring together crystals that include intense lapis lazuli and gray-blue celestite.

✦ **VIOLET CRYSTALS** (pages 96-105) vary from lilac lepidolite to vibrant amethyst.

✦ **RAINBOW CRYSTALS** (pages 106-115) present iridescent labradorite and watermelon tourmaline.

✦ **MULTICOLORED CRYSTALS** (pages 116-125) introduce calcite rocks and pretty banded fluorites.

✦ **WHITE AND CLEAR CRYSTALS** (pages 126-135) range from ice-white diamond to shadowy phantom quartz.

✦ **BLACK AND GRAY CRYSTALS** (pages 136-145) include lustrous silver and rich, black jet.

✦ **BROWN CRYSTALS** (pages 147-155) vary from hazel-and-black chiastolite to ginger-colored aragonite.

What Are Crystals?

Crystals are formed from minerals, and they occur naturally in the Earth's surface. Under the microscope, a crystal's atomic structure resembles a three-dimensional lattice. Every crystal's atomic pattern is unique.

Naturally occurring crystals appear in several fixed crystalline shapes: single crystals, clusters or geodes (hollow rocks with crystals growing toward the center), rough rocks, pebbles and alluvial crystals. Crystals shaped by artist or machine can take any form, and are often beautifully polished.

Crystals refer to many types of mineral. Abalone shell (below) is still referred to as a crystal although it does not have a crystalline structure.

Titanium quartz cluster (above)

· Crystal Centerpieces ·

Large, beautiful crystals, often called crystal centerpieces, can be powerful enough to change the energy of an entire room, benefiting every person, animal and plant. These are great in living rooms, or any area where people gather, as they exude a positive energy that encourages everyone to feel more relaxed. The most common crystal centerpieces are geodes, large rocks of rose quartz and amethyst and quartz crystal clusters.

· Living Crystals ·

Crystals predate DNA as the building blocks of life. In fact, as Professor Richard Dawkins explains in his book *The Selfish Gene*, crystals may have been the original life form on Earth. Human beings are made up of many tiny microscopic crystals – most enzymes and many other biochemical structures within cells are in fact crystals.

I have found that anyone working with crystals will, over time, come to appreciate them as live objects – some become lifelong friends, whereas others will come and go as they are needed. For this reason, I do avoid the term 'use' in relation to crystals. As we don't 'use' people, we wouldn't 'use' crystals. So whenever the term 'work with' appears throughout this book, it refers to carrying, wearing, placing or holding a crystal in whichever way is recommended.

Out of This World

Meteorite and tektite are the only natural crystals included in this book that are not formed in the Earth's crust. Meteorite is created in outer space, and tektite is formed when meteorites explode on impact with the Earth, liquefying the surface and fusing with it. There are also a few crystals created artificially using natural minerals and crystals, such as angel aura and titanium quartz.

Meteorite　　　**Tektite**

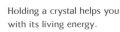

Holding a crystal helps you with its living energy.

How Crystals Work

Crystals may work as if by magic, but there are a multitude of reasons as to how and why these enigmatic stones are thought to possess the ability to heal and to magnify energy.

It is certain that crystals vibrate, and that they exhibit piezoelectric and pyroelectric properties. The piezoelectric effect is the ability of crystals to generate a voltage in response to mechanical stress; the pyroelectric effect is a crystal's ability to generate an electrical potential in response to temperature change.

In terms of their application, crystals provide the movement for quartz watches, and they are also used for igniting the flame of some gas lighters such as cigarette lighters. Crystals also hold heat and electricity,

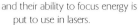

and their ability to focus energy is put to use in lasers.

As a crystal healer, I believe that crystals have an innate energy that can benefit you, those around you, and your home and workspace. They may improve your general state of wellbeing, dispel negative energy and speed up positive changes in your life. If magic is defined as that which is beyond our understanding at this point in time, then crystals are certainly magical.

Amber can help sharpen
your memory.

Bloodstone can help your
body eliminate toxins.

Hold chrysoprase to
improve dexterity.

· The Effect of Crystals ·

The healing, life-enhancing powers of crystals
have been recorded in many ancient texts, from
the Bible to traditional Chinese medical texts and
Ayurvedic and Ancient Egyptian teachings. But
how may crystals affect you individually, in terms
of your emotional response? Because we're all
different – as are crystals – it's impossible to
describe the precise response you may have to a
crystal. However, in my experience, understanding
the process of healing is certainly helpful. In crystal
healing workshops, here's how I explain the effect
of crystals when you work with them for healing.

Imagine a traditional set of weighing scales,
unevenly balanced with one side higher than the
other. Visualize a weight dropped onto this side
to bring it into balance with the other one. The
scales wobble a little as they find equilibrium but

Place a Herkimer
diamond under
your pillow for
a restful night's
sleep.

soon come to rest at their point of balance.
When you work with crystals, the same can
happen to you, your emotions wobbling before
stabilizing. The effect of crystals can feel
uncomfortable as you release negative thoughts
and emotions, but persevere and you will soon
notice improvements in your life.

Choosing Crystals

Always choose crystals that particularly appeal to you. These are the ones you find pretty, sparkly or interesting, and keep you going back to them.

When you check information on a specific crystal, it may be obvious why you are drawn to it – perhaps it offers benefits that you, or someone close to you, needs at the present time. Even if the purpose of the crystal is not yet clear, usually it will be revealed in due course; if you don't need the qualities of a particular stone now, it's likely that you will later. The most important aspect of choosing a crystal is to trust your gut instinct, your first response.

As you look around a store or at a display, keep in mind the reason you are searching for a crystal. If the crystal is to be a gift, think about the person you are choosing for. The right crystal will catch your eye and hold your attention. Take this book with you on crystal expeditions so that you can look up the crystal in the color sections to find out what it does.

· The Pendulum Method ·

A natural and ancient human ability, dowsing is possibly the oldest form of divination. It's a simple skill to learn, and is an easy way to select crystals for yourself or for other people, even those you don't know well.

Scrying with Crystals

Scrying is a method of predicting the future or seeing the past by staring into a quartz crystal ball or an obsidian mirror. The energies of apophyllite and rainbow obsidian promote this ability. There are many other methods of crystal divination, but perhaps the most common way of linking to the future with crystals is in their selection. Sometimes you may be drawn to a crystal that you don't really need at that moment – take it, as it will become beneficial in the future.

Choose a pendulum and ask it a simple question to which you know the answer is yes, such as, 'Am I a woman?' or 'Am I a man?'. The pendulum will move, perhaps in a clockwise or counterclockwise circle, backward and forward or side to side. This is your 'yes' response. Then ask the opposite question and the pendulum will exhibit a different movement, which is your 'no' response. Hold your pendulum over each crystal and ask, 'Do I need this crystal?' It's that simple. You can then look the crystal up in this book to find how it can help you.

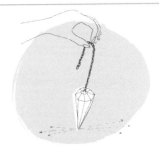 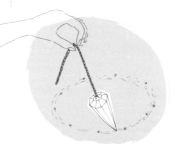

Often a pendulum will move backward and forward or in a circular motion. By asking the pendulum to show you its 'yes' and 'no' response, you can ascertain which movement means yes and no when you ask a question.

Cleansing Crystals

Crystals may need cleansing because they pick up energy and get dusty, particularly as crystals' electromagnetic charge makes dust adhere to their surfaces.

Crystals absorb energy from their surroundings, and also from anyone, or anything, that has touched them. Over time, they can lose their sparkle, brightness and even color; they may also feel sticky to touch. When you see these changes in your crystals, you know that it's time to cleanse them to refresh their natural energies.

Here are some of the many ways to cleanse your crystals before you work with them. With all of these methods, your intention is key. As you cleanse your crystals, focus on the task in hand and, in your mind, ask that all old or negative energies be released.

A singing bowl can be used to cleanse crystals with sound.

RUNNING WATER Most crystals can simply be washed under running water, with intent – focus your mind on effective cleansing as you hold the crystal under water for a few minutes. Holding a crystal under a fresh running stream is ideal, but running tap water is just fine, too. If your crystal is water-soluble, such as halite, use one of the alternative methods to cleanse it of stale energy.

rituals. Waft the cleansing smoke over the crystal – traditionally, this is done with a feather. Then safely extinguish the smudge stick after use. If you extinguish it in a pot of sand, it's easy to relight and use again.

BREATH Breathing on your crystal has a cleansing effect. Breathe in deeply then, as you exhale, focus your mind on cleansing the crystal of any negativity.

Quartz cluster

SUNLIGHT Leave the crystal in sunlight, although beware that quartz crystals, especially crystal balls, will focus the Sun's rays and can be a fire risk.

MOONLIGHT Place the crystal where it will be lit by the Moon, especially a full or a new Moon. A waxing Moon symbolizes a phase of increasing energy, whereas a waning Moon is linked with declining energy, so will not cleanse your crystal effectively.

INCENSE Waft the smoke from a frankincense or sandalwood incense stick over the crystal.

SMUDGING LIGHT a smudge stick that contains sage over the crystal – sage is traditionally used in Native American cleansing

EARTH Bury your crystal in the ground when the Moon is full and unearth it at the time of a new Moon.

AMETHYST BED, QUARTZ CLUSTER OR GEODE Place the crystal on an amethyst bed or quartz cluster, or inside a geode.

SOUND To clear crystals of any unhelpful vibrations, the sounds created by chanting, drumming, Tibetan bells or cymbals (known as tingshaw) are effective.

REIKI Practicing reiki on your crystals is also a good method of cleansing.

Placing Crystals at Home or at Work

You can choose to simply place your crystals around your home and work place, perhaps on your desk, or create a personal sacred space just for you and your crystals.

Creating a special, life-enhancing space where you can work with your crystals – for example, through meditation – is both beneficial and fun. The space may be a desk at work or your entire home and it may be permanent or temporary. Here's how to go about it.

Creating a Special Space at Home

I Begin by taking a little time to clear out unwanted clutter, from old newspapers and magazines to any unwanted, broken or unloved items. This is a great opportunity to discard any junk you've been hoarding.

2 Clean the space thoroughly. Open the windows and air the room.

3 Make a list of all the aspects of your life that are important to you – for example, your love life, your friendships, your career, your creativity, and so on. Select crystals that represent these aspects and bring the benefits you want. Your focus might be on what you would like to change in your life. For example, you might choose ruby if you want more passion in a relationship, or spirit quartz if you would like to bond more closely with colleagues at work.

4 Place the crystals around the room as you see fit – remember, it's your space. Choose some relaxing music, light candles and incense if you wish, then sit quietly for a while in your special space.

Crystals for Your Space

The following list gives an idea of what crystals might be chosen for special a space. These crystals work well together to bring a range of benefits:

✦ **PERIDOT** to clear emotional blockages, leading to a release of unhelpful energy and situations in your life. This crystal gives you the impetus to start that big clear-out of clutter.

✦ **QUARTZ** to bring positive energy into a space.

✦ **AMETHYST** to create the calm, relaxing atmosphere that will encourage you to feel at home.

✦ **ROSE QUARTZ** to allow love to flow into your life and home.

✦ **CITRINE** to encourage fun, happiness and abundance.

Healing with Crystals

When placed on the body's chakra points, or energy centers, crystals can help promote physical, spiritual and emotional healing.

Chakra is a Sanskrit word that means 'wheel'. The energy centers in the body appear like wheels or balls to those who see energy – hence the name. Most Eastern traditions describe a system of seven chakras, with each correlating to a different part of the body.

Chakras can become out of balance, affecting wellbeing. Placing crystals on the chakras focuses energy directly where needed for healing. Crystals can also be placed on specific areas to help ease pain or discomfort.

When all chakras are balanced, many benefits can be felt. A healthy chakra is in balance and full of moving energy. Where there is dis-ease, the energy slows or becomes blocked. Working with chakras can heal and prevent dis-ease, promoting physical, mental and spiritual health.

Chakras and Their Meanings

CROWN spirituality, connection to the universe, imagination and awareness

BROW mind, ideas, thoughts, dreams, psychic abilities

THROAT communication

HEART safety, trust, adventure and love

SOLAR PLEXUS personal power, emotions, physical center

SACRAL connection to other people, creativity and energy

BASE survival, health, abundance, connection to the Earth, moving forward in life

Locating the Chakras

7 CROWN top of the head

6 BROW center of forehead, above the eyebrows (also known as the third eye)

5 THROAT center of the throat

4 HEART center of the chest

3 SOLAR PLEXUS behind the soft cartilage at bottom of the breastbone

2 SACRAL just below the navel

1 BASE the coccyx at the base of the spine

7 CROWN Amethyst

6 BROW Lapis Lazuli

5 THROAT Blue Lace Agate

4 HEART Malachite

3 SOLAR PLEXUS Citrine

2 SACRAL Carnelian

1 BASE Red Jasper

Lie down and place the crystals suggested here (see right) on your chakras. Lie still for 30 minutes, rest and relax. Ideally, repeat this exercise daily.

Crystals on the Move

Most smaller crystals can be carried or worn, so as you travel, you'll benefit from the healing qualities of the crystals you choose for each day. There's even a crystal to ease travel stress — turquoise in your bag can help with the daily commute.

· Carrying Crystals ·

This is one of the simplest ways of working with crystals and allows you to have several with you at any time. Put them in your pocket or place them in a drawstring pouch tied to your belt or other convenient item. Keep them in your wallet, purse or bag (citrine is a great crystal to have in your wallet at all times, because it attracts wealth!). Take them out regularly to hold or rub them, or to place them on your body for healing (see pages 18–19).

·Wearing Crystals ·

Crystals have been worn throughout history, treasured for their beauty and power. The remains of crystal jewelry have been found in ancient graves around the world. Wearing crystals gives you the benefit of decorative adornment while having their beneficial energies constantly near you.

It's also worth considering how you wear crystal jewelry. A short pendant or choker will fall on the throat area, which is also the location of the throat chakra (see page 19) – so you might like to choose a crystal linked with communication and the color blue, which are this chakra's attributes. Wearing a lapis lazuli choker or short pendant, for example, will help you express yourself, so this would be the perfect item to choose on a day when being understood is important. Presentations, meetings and interviews will all benefit from 'true blue' throat chakra crystals.

· Giving Crystals as Gifts ·

Crystals make perfect gifts for all occasions. You can give birthstones to anyone at anytime and they make a lovely gift to mark a child's birth. You can select crystals for weddings, anniversaries, birthdays and house warmings, or to say 'Thank you', 'I love you', 'Sorry' or 'Get well soon'. Think carefully about the recipient of a crystal while you are making your selection to be sure that you pick the right one.

Wearing Your Totem Animal

Many cultures around the world believe in the power of animal spirits or energies. Some come and go, marking phases in your life, while others 'walk by your side' throughout life. You can often identify these for yourself by the type of animal you like, the pets you have chosen to keep and the animal pictures that appeal to you. Sometimes our pets are a representation of a wild animal. For example, often people who have a German Shepherd dog have a wolf as one of their totem animals. Animal energies bring out our character and natural abilities. Crystals such as stibnite help to connect us to this power.

Stibnite, for connection with our totem animals

Meditating with Crystals

Crystals can help you to focus and clear the mind for meditation. Regular meditation with crystals will help your mind unwind, and also bring more energy and creativity to your thoughts.

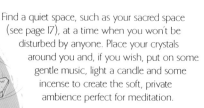

Find a quiet space, such as your sacred space (see page 17), at a time when you won't be disturbed by anyone. Place your crystals around you and, if you wish, put on some gentle music, light a candle and some incense to create the soft, private ambience perfect for meditation.

1 Relax by breathing slowly and deeply so that you become centered and calm. Focus on your breathing as you inhale and exhale, letting go of tension and day-to-day thoughts.

2 Choose one crystal to focus on and allow yourself to explore it with all your senses. Feel its

facets and look carefully at it. Hold it closely and examine it, then place it down before you. Notice its surfaces, colors and textures.

3 Now pick up the crystal and hold it in both hands, or let your hands play with the crystal, passing it between both your palms. Close your eyes and connect with the crystal.

Meditating with sunstone brings the Sun's energy into mind and body.

Crystals and Spirit Guides

Crystals can help us connect to our spirit guides. These may be deceased family members, wise people from another time or simply energy spirits. They give a helping hand when needed, provide comfort, and supply us with answers that seem to appear out of thin air. When you first start to see spirits, they often materialize as blue balls of light floating near you or you may just sense their presence. Meditating with morganite or sapphire can promote this link.

Sapphire   Morganite

4 Be aware of any sensations you experience – physical, emotional, mental and spiritual. Stay with this process for about 10 minutes minimum, or longer if you have the time.

Daily meditation with your crystals helps you find space within a busy life, and gain perspective on everyday worries. It will open your mind to new possibilities and give you a different, more positive view of life.

Elixirs

A crystal elixir is, literally, crystal water – a way of taking the energies of crystals directly into your body, which can be very beneficial.

Most crystal elixirs can be drunk, just as a glass of water, or applied topically to the skin. Not all crystals make safe elixirs (see the Caution box, opposite), so do take care when choosing a crystal for an elixir. All you need to make an elixir is your chosen crystal, a bowl or glass and some fresh water.

· How to Make an Elixir ·

1 Focusing your intent on the purpose of the elixir, cleanse your crystal. Cleanse it under running water. As you cleanse, think about the benefits you would like from the elixir.
2 Next, place the crystal in a container of water. Ideally, use distilled water or water from a pure source, such as spring water, but you can still use tap water if you don't have any other alternatives. Cover the container and leave it overnight in the refrigerator.
3 Drink the elixir or apply topically over the next 24 hours. Discard any leftover elixir after this period of time.

Some people like to enhance elixirs in sunlight or moonlight, or by surrounding them with quartz crystals.

CAUTION Not all crystals are suitable for elixirs. Of the crystals included in this book, do not use halite, crocoite, vanadinite, fuchsite or erythrite; and do not make an elixir of meteorite if it is a chondrite or an achondrite. If you are in doubt, consult your crystal healer.

◆ Rose quartz elixir, applied to the skin as a tonic, can freshen up a tired, dull complexion.

· Elixirs to Try ·

◆ Drinking an elixir of aragonite can help soothe aching muscles.

◆ Soothe tired eyes by bathing them in an elixir of blue lace agate.

◆ Bathe minor cuts and grazes with an elixir of amber or carnelian, which act as a mild antiseptic.

◆ For shiny hair, after washing, rinse with an elixir of moonstone or jade, and massage into the scalp.

◆ Pink opal elixir helps with mental unrest, restoring a sense of peace and calm.

◆ A hematite elixir, applied directly to the skin, can help to soothe the discomfort of sunburn.

Birthstones

It is said that carrying your birthstone connects you with the vibration of the universe as it was when you were born. This brings protection, good fortune, health and longevity.

The idea of birthstones goes back millennia. However, birthstones can be confusing, as a number of different crystals are associated with each of the zodiac signs and often one crystal is linked to several signs. Crystals can also be linked to particular months and seasons. There are over 2,000 different minerals on the Earth, and only 12 star signs.

Crystals have been linked to months and zodiac signs through mystical interpretations in the Bible, by the Chaldeans (see box, opposite) and in the Hindu, Ancient Egyptian, Chinese and Native American traditions. These ancient writings and oracles differ, partly due to the local availability of different types of crystal and partly due to local beliefs and culture.

The Chaldeans

One of the earliest written records of the association between crystals and astrology came from the Chaldeans, people who lived in Mesopotamia around 4000BCE.

Famous for studying the stars to foretell the future, they linked the following planets and gems:

SATURN	Sapphire
JUPITER	Zircon
SUN	Diamond
MARS	Ruby
VENUS	Emerald
MERCURY	Agate
MOON	Selenite

The planets Uranus, Neptune and Pluto were yet to be discovered.

Birthstone Crystals

CAPRICORN garnet

AQUARIUS amethyst

PISCES aquamarine

ARIES red jasper

TAURUS rose quartz

GEMINI citrine

CANCER moonstone

LEO carnelian

VIRGO peridot

LIBRA kyanite

SCORPIO malachite

SAGITTARIUS sodalite

Red 30

Orange 40

Yellow 50

Green 60

Pink 74

Blue 84

'Crystal' comes from the Greek 'krystallos'

Crystals by Color

Violet 96

Rainbow 106

Multicolored 116

White and
Clear 126

Black and
Gray 136

Brown 146

Here are 101 crystals, arranged by their common
color. Enjoy the process of discovering more about
your crystals, and about those crystals you might like
to work with now and in the future.

Red

Spinel 32 • Red jasper 33

Zircon 34 • Garnet 35

Ruby 36

•

Mookaite 37

•

Falcon's eye 38

•

Red calcite 39

Red crystals give you the courage to move forward in life

Spinel

Energizing spinel releases the true inner you, bringing warmth to relationships

STAR SIGN Sagittarius

PLANET Jupiter

ELEMENT fire

CHAKRA base

· CRYSTAL TIPS ·

Carry spinel and rub it when you feel tired to re-energize
yourself physically, emotionally, mentally and spiritually

✦

Keep spinel with you to allow your inner beauty to shine
so others can see who you really are

✦

Put spinel around your home to encourage
lasting relationships

✦

Place spinel under your pillow at night to
promote longevity

✦

Work with spinel to
release your true personality

✦

Red jasper

STAR SIGN Aries

PLANET Mars

ELEMENT fire

CHAKRA base

· CRYSTAL TIPS ·

Place red jasper at the foot of your bed to increase passion
and liven up your sex life

✦

Put red jasper under your pillow to help you remember
your dreams

✦

Carry or wear red jasper to prevent you from catching winter
colds and flu

✦

Hold red jasper to find a new way of doing something
or to understand a new idea

✦

Meditate within a circle of red jasper to create
a focused environment

✦

Passion-igniting red jasper promotes purpose

Zircon

STAR SIGN Leo

PLANET Sun

ELEMENT fire

CHAKRA base

· CRYSTAL TIPS ·

Carry zircon to enhance your relationship — give one to your partner too

✦

Put zircon under your pillow to help relieve insomnia and bring you a peaceful night's sleep

✦

Hold zircon to calm you when you feel stressed

✦

Place zircon around the home to lift depression

✦

Carry zircon to boost your personal magnetism

✦

Hold zircon to the affected area to relieve an allergic reaction

✦

Healing zircon brings peace and comfort

Garnet

STAR SIGN Capricorn

PLANET Saturn

ELEMENT fire

CHAKRA heart

· CRYSTAL TIPS ·

Wear garnet to boost your vitality and make you
more attractive to the opposite sex

✦

Put a garnet crystal in your purse or wallet
to attract abundance

✦

Place garnet at the head of your bed to ease depression

✦

Carry garnet to reduce chaos in your life

✦

Wear a garnet bracelet on your left wrist to draw
spiritual ideas to you; wear it on your right wrist
to create change in your life

✦

Life-enhancing garnet creates positive change

Ruby

STAR SIGN Sagittarius

PLANET Mars

ELEMENT fire

CHAKRA heart

Strengthening ruby helps you make decisions for magical change and wondrous new beginnings

· CRYSTAL TIPS ·

Wear ruby to increase passion

◆

Carry or wear ruby if you are pregnant to promote
the healthy development of your baby

◆

Place ruby near your bed to promote health and healing

◆

Carry ruby to balance the menstrual cycle and
ease discomfort

◆

Put a ruby in your bag or pocket to attract wealth

◆

Hold ruby to speed your thought processes

◆

Mookaite

STAR SIGN Leo

PLANET Sun

ELEMENT fire

CHAKRA base

· CRYSTAL TIPS ·

Place mookaite around the home to encourage good
behavior from children

◆

Take mookaite to job interviews to increase your confidence

◆

Carry mookaite to promote weight loss

◆

Hold mookaite to help you make the right decision

◆

Keep mookaite in your work area to inspire you
if you are a creative artist

◆

Hold mookaite for comfort if you
are feeling lonely

◆

Balancing mookaite enhances communication and good outcomes

Falcon's eye

STAR SIGN Capricorn

PLANET Saturn

ELEMENT earth

CHAKRA base

· CRYSTAL TIPS ·

Put falcon's eye in your pocket to help you carry out practical tasks more efficiently

✦

Keep falcon's eye under your bed to boost your sexuality

✦

Hold a piece of falcon's eye to the affected area for relief from sunburn

✦

Carry falcon's eye to help you control your emotions

✦

Lie down quietly and place falcon's eye on your navel if you are trying to get pregnant

✦

Strengthening falcon's eye offers practical help

Red calcite

STAR SIGN Cancer

PLANET Moon

ELEMENT water

CHAKRA base

· CRYSTAL TIPS ·

Hold red calcite to help you relax if you are trying to do too much and be in too many places at the same time

◆

Put red calcite near overactive children to calm their behavior

◆

Place red calcite next to your bed to prevent you from repeating negative patterns

◆

Hold red calcite for comfort when you feel panicky

◆

Keep red calcite near you to boost your emotional energy

◆

Calming red calcite enhances positive self-image

Orange

Orange calcite 42

Spessartine 43

Halite 44

Carnelian 45

Wulfenite 46

Sunstone 47

Vanadinite 48

Crocoite 49

Orange crystals bring the vibrant energy of the Sun's rays

Orange calcite

STAR SIGN Leo

PLANET Sun

ELEMENT fire

CHAKRA sacral

· CRYSTAL TIPS ·

Place orange calcite under your bed to
boost vitality throughout the next day

◆

Hold orange calcite to balance your energies

◆

Keep orange calcite with you to bring calmness and tranquillity

◆

Put orange calcite in your workplace to reduce
tension between colleagues

◆

Carry orange calcite with you to
inspire you throughout the day

◆

Meditate with orange calcite to let its
energy bring sunshine into your life

◆

Orange calcite provides warmth
and emotional healing

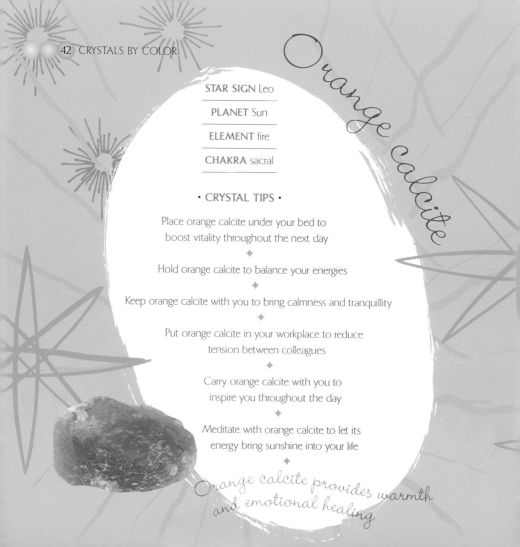

Spessartine

STAR SIGN Aquarius

PLANET Uranus

ELEMENT air

CHAKRA sacral

· CRYSTAL TIPS ·

Hold spessartine to enhance your ability to analyze situations

✦

Place spessartine around you to boost vitality

✦

Hold spessartine to clear your mind of clutter
and allow your thoughts to form clearly

✦

Carry or wear spessartine to bring you emotional balance

✦

Keep spessartine with you to give you the courage
to make important life changes

✦

Put spessartine under your pillow to encourage
your mind to let go of worry at night

✦

*Life-enhancing spessartine increases
energy and sets the mind ready for action*

Halite

STAR SIGN Cancer

PLANET Moon

ELEMENT water

CHAKRA sacral

Longer-lasting halite boosts endurance

· CRYSTAL TIPS ·

Carry halite to give you the stamina for arduous tasks

◆

Hold halite to swollen areas of your body to relieve
water retention

◆

Put a piece of halite in each of the places where you spend time
to reduce mood swings

◆

Take halite with you when eating out because it can help
prevent you from getting an upset stomach

◆

Hold halite in the palm of your hand to regain your
balance when contaminated by other people's energy

◆

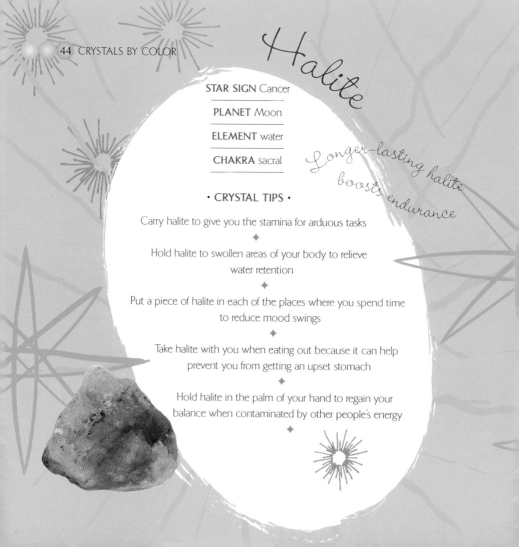

Carnelian

STAR SIGN Leo

PLANET Sun

ELEMENT fire

CHAKRA sacral

· CRYSTAL TIPS ·

Hold carnelian – the super energy stone – when
you need a boost

◆

Put carnelian in your pocket to benefit from its power
if you are giving a presentation or lecture, or you are
a musician performing live

Carry or wear carnelian to energize you when you have a cold

◆

Place carnelian around your home when you need
to improve your self-esteem

◆

Take carnelian with you on retreats to keep you
energized and focused

◆

Revitalize with invigorating 'feel-better' carnelian

Wulfenite

STAR SIGN Sagittarius

PLANET Jupiter

ELEMENT fire

CHAKRA heart

• **CRYSTAL TIPS** •

Place wulfenite around your bed to prolong youthfulness

✦

Focus on a wulfenite crystal cluster each night
before you go to sleep to help you find the
path to your soul mate

✦

Meditate with wulfenite to connect with your higher self

✦

Keep wulfenite crystals around you to promote
magic in your life

✦

Work with wulfenite to recognize and
come to terms with your dark side

✦

Hold wulfenite to help you contact
your spirit guide

✦

*Wulfenite promotes a heightened awareness,
allowing you to see the world from a new perspective*

Sunstone

STAR SIGN	Leo
PLANET	Sun
ELEMENT	fire
CHAKRA	crown

· CRYSTAL TIPS ·

Keep sunstone near you to see the brighter side of life

◆

Put sunstone in your purse or wallet to
bring you abundance

◆

Hold sunstone to ease away fear when you are scared

◆

Wear sunstone, the 'ghost buster', to keep away bad spirits

◆

Add some sunstone crystals to a bowl of warm water
to soothe aching feet

◆

The energy of sunstone brings health, wealth and happiness

Vanadinite

STAR SIGN Virgo

PLANET Mercury

ELEMENT earth

CHAKRA sacral

· CRYSTAL TIPS ·

Keep vanadinite around you for strength of purpose when
you are working toward a goal

✦

Put vanadinite in your purse or wallet to encourage thrift if you
have a habit of overspending

✦

Hold vanadinite to relieve the feeling of exhaustion
when you have done too much

✦

Carry vanadinite to promote easy breathing if you
suffer from asthma

✦

Light a candle and place several vanadinite crystal
clusters around you to create a perfect space
for meditation

✦

Invigorating vanadinite brings a breath of fresh air

Crocoite

STAR SIGN Aries

PLANET Mars

ELEMENT fire

CHAKRA sacral

· CRYSTAL TIPS ·

Keep crocoite – the 'divorce stone' – near you to guide you through a divorce and help ease the trauma

◆

Place crocoite near the head of your bed to boost intuition

◆

Place crocoite by the foot of your bed to increase your sexuality

◆

Put crocoite on your desk at work to enhance creativity

◆

Carry a single crocoite crystal to help boost your stamina during life-changing situations

◆

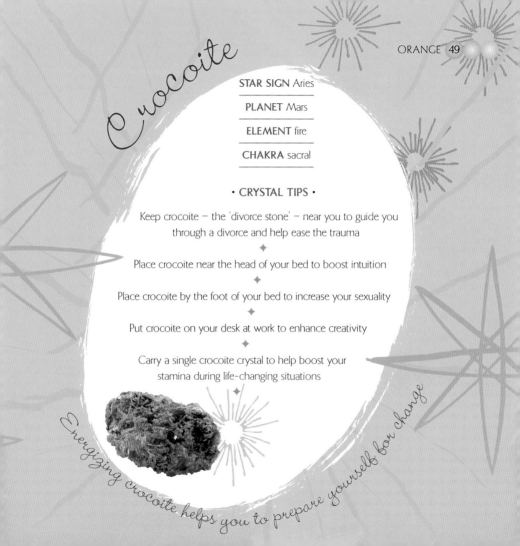

Energizing crocoite helps you to prepare yourself for change

Yellow crystals stimulate creative energy and courage

Yellow

Tiger's eye 52

Citrine 53

Apatite 54

Yellow fluorite 55

Gold 56

Copper 57

Imperial topaz 58

Amber 59

Tiger's eye

STAR SIGN Capricorn

PLANET Saturn

ELEMENT earth

CHAKRA solar plexus

· CRYSTAL TIPS ·

Hold tiger's eye when you are dithering for that
special 'go-for-it' feeling

✦

Put tiger's eye in your purse or wallet and it will never be empty

✦

Wear or carry tiger's eye to improve your intuition

✦

Place tiger's eye around your home to protect it and your
family from negativity and fear

✦

Keep tiger's eye near you to promote new beginnings and give
you the courage to move forward in life

✦

Strengthening tiger's eye
promotes the boldness
associated with the tiger

Citrine

STAR SIGN Gemini

PLANET Mercury

ELEMENT air

CHAKRA solar plexus

· CRYSTAL TIPS ·

Put a piece of citrine in your purse or wallet to bring you abundance
and wealth – it is known as the 'money stone'

◆

Keep citrine at work to boost your creativity

◆

Wear citrine when you are low to make you feel brighter

◆

Citrine in your bedroom enhances your relationships

◆

Hold citrine to prevent nausea and stomachache

◆

Place citrine crystals in every room to speed
up the sale of a house

◆

Uplifting citrine brightens your life with positive energy

Apatite

STAR SIGN Gemini

PLANET Mercury

ELEMENT air

CHAKRA throat

· CRYSTAL TIPS ·

Keep apatite near you if you are a writer, performer or
communicator to stimulate creativity

◆

Carry or wear apatite to encourage weight loss

◆

Drink an apatite elixir (see page 24) for emotional or physical healing

◆

Meditate with apatite to find your inner self

◆

Place apatite around your home to dispel negativity,
and to support the balance of male and female energies
for a tranquil living space

◆

Work with apatite to recall
past lives

◆

Balancing apatite promotes health and a sense of wellbeing

Yellow fluorite

STAR SIGN Leo	
PLANET Sun	
ELEMENT fire	
CHAKRA sacral	

· CRYSTAL TIPS ·

Put yellow fluorite in the center of a group to create a positive dynamic

✦

Wear or carry yellow fluorite to promote weight loss, and to
dispel toxins from mind and body

✦

Hold yellow fluorite to enhance creativity and the flow of ideas

✦

Lie down and place yellow fluorite on your brow chakra to clear
your mind of negative thoughts and worries

✦

Place yellow fluorite in your hall to draw
spiritual energy into your home

✦

Energizing yellow fluorite stimulates the creative mind

Gold

STAR SIGN Leo	
PLANET Sun	
ELEMENT fire	
CHAKRA heart	

• CRYSTAL TIPS •

Wear gold to help you reach your true potential

✦

Carry gold to dispel toxins from mind and body

✦

Hold gold to release anger and pride, allowing you to let
go of negativity and depressive thoughts and feelings

✦

Put gold under your pillow to prevent you from having nightmares

✦

Place gold near you to draw healing energy toward you when
you are feeling ill

✦

Meditate with gold to connect spiritually to the
universe and its infinite wisdom

✦

*Empowering gold connects you to the universal
flow of knowledge*

Copper

STAR SIGN Taurus

PLANET Venus

ELEMENT earth

CHAKRA sacral

· CRYSTAL TIPS ·

Carry or wear copper for a feeling of wellbeing

◆

Hold copper to help you find lost property

◆

Place copper in your home or workplace to calm overexcitability

◆

Work with copper to boost your chi, strengthening your inner self

◆

Hold copper in the morning after eating or drinking to excess –
it can stimulate your metabolism and speed the elimination
of toxins from your body

◆

Keep copper with you to revitalize you when
feeling exhausted

◆

Invigorating 'feel-better' copper boosts the flow of life-force energy

Imperial topaz

STAR SIGN Leo

PLANET Sun

ELEMENT fire

CHAKRA solar plexus

• CRYSTAL TIPS •

Wear imperial topaz to enhance your natural magnetism

✦

Hold imperial topaz to stimulate your mental energy, promoting
the flow of thoughts and ideas

✦

Meditate with imperial topaz to achieve a connection to the universe
and a feeling of oneness

✦

Place imperial topaz around your home to bring peace
and tranquillity

✦

Hold imperial topaz to help you relax

✦

Calming imperial topaz attracts life-enhancing energy

Amber

STAR SIGN Leo

PLANET Sun

ELEMENT fire

CHAKRA solar plexus

· CRYSTAL TIPS ·

Hold amber to boost your memory if you are forgetful

✦

Wear amber to purify your body, mind and spirit

✦

Burn amber as an incense to purify rooms and spaces

✦

Wear amber to bring you good luck and protect you from
negative energies

✦

Hold amber in your right hand to help you to release emotion
and focus your mind

✦

Give amber to your loved one to symbolize the
renewal of marriage vows

✦

Lucky amber is symbolic of love and good memories

Green

Jade 62

Bloodstone 63

Fuchsite 64

Aventurine 65

Malachite 66

Unakite 67

Green calcite 68

Emerald 69

Dioptase 70

Chrysoprase 71

Peridot 72

Amazonite 73

Green crystals promote serenity, health and wisdom

Jade

STAR SIGN Taurus

PLANET Venus

ELEMENT earth

CHAKRA heart

• CRYSTAL TIPS •

Hold jade to bring you answers to your problems

◆

Keep jade with you to help prevent accidents from occurring

◆

Hold jade then focus your mind on your ideals and on the inner strength required to achieve your goals

◆

Place jade under your pillow to promote dreaming and dream recall

◆

Wear jade to bring you inner peace

◆

Meditate with jade to find wisdom

◆

Give jade to a child to bring health, wealth and longevity

◆

Wisdom-enhancing jade protects you from harm

Bloodstone

STAR SIGN Aries

PLANET Mars

ELEMENT fire

CHAKRA heart

· CRYSTAL TIPS ·

Place bloodstone under your bed to wake up feeling
refreshed with a zest for life

✦

Keep bloodstone around you to relieve stress and help you to let
go of anger

✦

Wear bloodstone when you need strength and courage

✦

Hold bloodstone for inner strength when you
are feeling anxious

✦

Set bloodstone on your desk to enhance your abilities at work

✦

Carry bloodstone to encourage your body to eliminate toxins

✦

*Invigorating bloodstone energizes the mind and body,
promoting the release of worries and other negative emotions*

Fuchsite

STAR SIGN Aquarius

PLANET Uranus

ELEMENT air

CHAKRA heart

· CRYSTAL TIPS ·

Keep fuchsite around you to speed recovery from illness

✦

Hold fuchsite to any affected areas of your skin to help clear up
eczema and other skin conditions

✦

Position fuchsite next to you at night to relieve feelings of unrequited love

✦

Place fuchsite throughout your home to benefit from its calming energy

✦

Hold fuchsite to help heal emotional wounds and assist emotional recovery

✦

Soothing fuchsite brings peace and tranquility

Aventurine

STAR SIGN Aries

PLANET Mars

ELEMENT fire

CHAKRA heart

· CRYSTAL TIPS ·

Hold aventurine to strained or aching muscles for relief

◆

Place aventurine around you when revising for or taking exams to ease your nerves and reduce stress

◆

Keep aventurine near you to benefit from increased reaction times when engaging in competitive sports or driving

◆

Carry aventurine to increase your leadership and motivational skills

◆

Wear aventurine to prevent 'energy vampires' from sapping your energy

◆

Meditate with aventurine to bring you closer to your spirit guide

◆

Relaxing aventurine helps you center your intent

Malachite

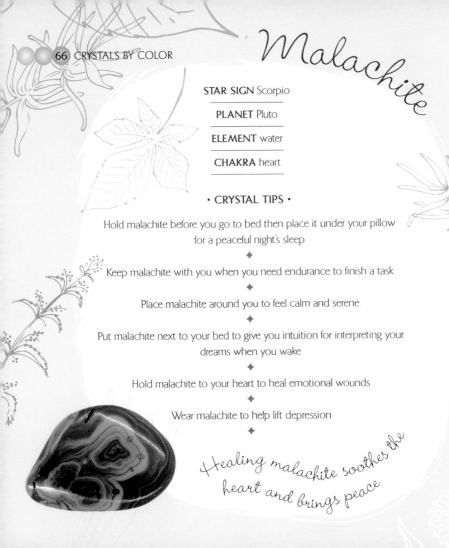

STAR SIGN Scorpio

PLANET Pluto

ELEMENT water

CHAKRA heart

· CRYSTAL TIPS ·

Hold malachite before you go to bed then place it under your pillow for a peaceful night's sleep

◆

Keep malachite with you when you need endurance to finish a task

◆

Place malachite around you to feel calm and serene

◆

Put malachite next to your bed to give you intuition for interpreting your dreams when you wake

◆

Hold malachite to your heart to heal emotional wounds

◆

Wear malachite to help lift depression

◆

Healing malachite soothes the heart and brings peace

Unakite

STAR SIGN Scorpio

PLANET Pluto

ELEMENT water

CHAKRA heart

· CRYSTAL TIPS ·

Carry unakite with you to overcome the blocks
you put in your own way

✦

Wear unakite to help you gain weight

✦

Keep unakite with you when pregnant to benefit your
health and that of your baby

✦

Meditate with unakite to discover more about your past lives

✦

Place unakite in your home to help you overcome grief associated
with the loss of a dream or an ideal

✦

*The red patches in unakite connect the base and heart
chakras and encourage action from the heart*

Green calcite

STAR SIGN Cancer

PLANET Moon

ELEMENT water

CHAKRA heart

· CRYSTAL TIPS ·

Carry or wear green calcite to help prevent you catching infections

✦

Place green calcite around you to calm your emotions

✦

Hold green calcite when you feel panicky

✦

Carry or hold green calcite to help you cope and not take offense
if other people laugh at your expense

✦

Hold green calcite to relieve stress

✦

Put green calcite on your bedside
table to help you relax
at night

✦

Calming green calcite helps you unwind, relieving the pressures and strains of life

Emerald

STAR SIGN Taurus

PLANET Venus

ELEMENT earth

CHAKRA heart

· CRYSTAL TIPS ·

Wear an emerald bracelet or ring to promote the qualities of patience
and honesty

◆

Hold emerald to calm you down when your temper rises and
you feel your blood boil

◆

Meditate with emerald to find your inner self

◆

Keep emerald near you to improve your memory

◆

Put emerald under your pillow to release feelings of jealousy

◆

Wear emerald near your heart to promote health

◆

Place emerald under your bed to increase fertility

◆

*Reviving emerald promotes kindness so you always
show your better side*

Dioptase

STAR SIGN Sagittarius

PLANET Jupiter

ELEMENT fire

CHAKRA all chakras

· CRYSTAL TIPS ·

Keep dioptase in your purse or wallet to attract wealth and abundance

✦

Place dioptase on your dining table to promote the balance of each diner's nutritional needs

✦

Put dioptase under your baby's crib to boost healthy development

✦

Place dioptase in your home to encourage positive change

✦

Hold dioptase to help you live in the present and experience life to the full

✦

Carry or wear dioptase for a healthy heart and circulation

✦

Healing dioptase brings positive energy to enhance mental and physical health

Chrysoprase

STAR SIGN Libra

PLANET Venus

ELEMENT air

CHAKRA heart

· CRYSTAL TIPS ·

Keep chrysoprase near you to clear the fog in your
mind when you are confused

◆

Hold chrysoprase to improve dexterity

◆

Carry or wear chrysoprase to lift your spirits when you are feeling low

◆

Place chrysoprase around you to create a meditative atmosphere

◆

Put chrysoprase under your pillow to help mend a broken heart

◆

Hold chrysoprase when you feel anxious or scared
– it will reduce stress and calm your fears

◆

Uplifting chrysoprase eases worry and brings clarity

Peridot

STAR SIGN Virgo

PLANET Mercury

ELEMENT earth

CHAKRA heart

· CRYSTAL TIPS ·

Keep peridot near to help you let go of pride

◆

Put peridot under your pillow to release emotional blockages

◆

Wear peridot to gain health and happiness from its energy

◆

Meditate with peridot to move forward on the path to enlightenment

◆

Carry peridot to help you detox on all levels: physical, emotional,
mental and spiritual

◆

Place peridot around your home to stimulate
activity and ward off laziness

◆

*Cleansing peridot washes away
the emotional grime of everyday living*

Amazonite

STAR SIGN Virgo

PLANET Mercury

ELEMENT earth

CHAKRA heart

· CRYSTAL TIPS ·

Hold amazonite to calm your nerves and bring peace if you are feeling troubled

◆

Keep amazonite near you to help you focus when studying or learning any new skill

◆

Wear or carry amazonite to boost your aura

◆

Place amazonite in your workplace to enhance creativity and stimulate the flow of ideas

◆

Carry amazonite when you feel low – it is a 'feel-good' stone

◆

The energy of amazonite keeps you calm and composed

Pink crystals warm the heart and soothe the soul

Pink

Kunzite 76

Rhodochrosite 77

Erythrite 78

Rhodonite 79

Pink opal 80

Rose quartz 81

Morganite 82

Eudialyte 83

Kunzite

STAR SIGN Taurus

PLANET Venus

ELEMENT earth

CHAKRA heart

· CRYSTAL TIPS ·

Carry or wear kunzite to help you express love

✦

Place kunzite in your home to remove negativity and
provide a protective energy shield

✦

Put kunzite under your bed to promote female sexuality

✦

Keep kunzite with you and hold it when you have withdrawal
pangs from smoking or any other addiction

✦

Carry kunzite to promote a youthful appearance

✦

Hold kunzite while meditating to speed
the centering of your being

Energizing kunzite helps remove obstacles

Rhodochrosite

STAR SIGN Leo

PLANET Sun

ELEMENT fire

CHAKRA heart

· CRYSTAL TIPS ·

Carry rhodochrosite to bring more passion into your world

✦

Place rhodochrosite around your bed to enhance your sex life

✦

Wear rhodochrosite to bring you courage in times of need

✦

Carry rhodochrosite and give it a rub when you are running around
trying to do too much and feeling stressed

✦

Hold rhodochrosite to bring you comfort in times of emotional trauma

✦

Keep rhodochrosite near you to promote happy
changes when your life is going well

✦

Rhodochrosite for passion!

Erythrite

STAR SIGN	Virgo
PLANET	Mercury
ELEMENT	earth
CHAKRA	throat

· CRYSTAL TIPS ·

Carry erythrite to enhance your communication skills

✦

Place erythrite in your home for a better perspective on your life and the world around you

✦

Hold erythrite to speed your recovery from illness

✦

Lie down and place erythrite on your body to help clear skin blemishes or hold it to your face, if required

✦

Hold erythrite to a sore throat to bring relief

✦

Purifying erythrite gives a clearer view of the world

Rhodonite

STAR SIGN Taurus

PLANET Venus

ELEMENT earth

CHAKRA heart

Peaceful rhodonite brings forth love

· CRYSTAL TIPS ·

Wear rhodonite to promote the flow of unconditional spiritual love toward those you care for

✦

Carry rhodonite with you to ground the feeling of love in your physical world

✦

Hold rhodonite to help you let go of anxiety and bring you peace of mind

✦

Keep rhodonite (and rhodochrosite, see page 77) around you to stimulate musical creativity

✦

Put rhodonite in your workplace to maintain your attention to detail

✦

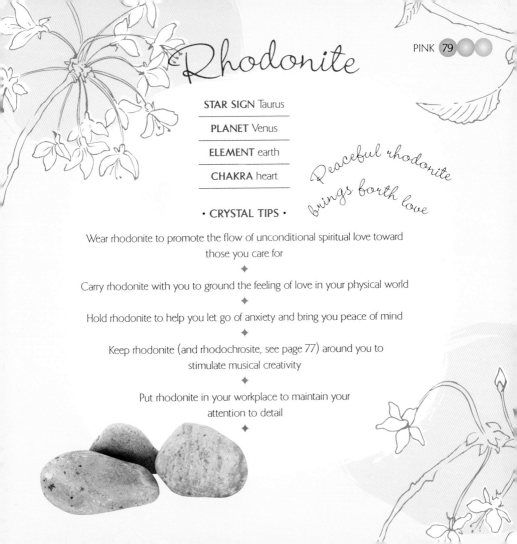

Pink opal

STAR SIGN Cancer

PLANET Moon

ELEMENT water

CHAKRA heart

· CRYSTAL TIPS ·

Carry pink opal to help you change your behavior patterns

✦

Put pink opal anywhere on your body to soothe your skin

✦

Meditate with pink opal to speed spiritual awakening

✦

Set pink opal throughout your home to help renew
relationships within the family

✦

Place pink opal in your bedroom to deepen
the love in your relationship

✦

Focus your thoughts on pink opal and
allow its energies to clear your mind

Calming pink opal enhances self-healing

Rose quartz

STAR SIGN Taurus

PLANET Venus

ELEMENT earth

CHAKRA heart

· **CRYSTAL TIPS** ·

Put several rose quartz in your bath to soothe your skin
and promote a youthful appearance

✦

Place rose quartz throughout your home and workplace and carry a small
crystal with you to promote love, romance and relationships

✦

Wear rose quartz to help ease general aches and pains

✦

Place rose quartz in your bedroom to balance your sex drive

✦

Use the energy of rose quartz to soothe
and calm yourself

✦

Rose quartz is a bubble bath for the emotions

Morganite

STAR SIGN Libra

PLANET Venus

ELEMENT air

CHAKRA heart

· CRYSTAL TIPS ·

Keep morganite with you to increase love in your life and
attract loving partners

◆

Place morganite under your pillow to allow your dreams to show you
your life from new angles

◆

Leave morganite in your home to promote a calm, embracing atmosphere

◆

Meditate with morganite to help find peace within
yourself through the wisdom of your spirit guides

◆

Carry morganite after a relationship breakup
to heal the sense of loss

◆

Comforting morganite fills the heart with love

Eudialyte

STAR SIGN Aries

PLANET Mars

ELEMENT fire

CHAKRA heart

· CRYSTAL TIPS ·

Place eudialyte on your eyelids to soothe sore or tired eyes

◆

Hold eudialyte to your heart to open your heart chakra and promote
emotional release

◆

Place eudialyte under your pillow to find and release issues from your past,
especially childhood, which are holding you back

◆

Carry eudialyte to enhance your extrasensory perception

◆

Meditate with eudialyte to help gain access to your past lives

◆

Eudialyte enhances spiritual understanding

Blue crystals promote spiritual awakening and serenity

Blue

Aquamarine 86

Sodalite 87

Cavansite 88

Lapis lazuli 89

Kyanite 90

Sapphire 91

Celestite 92

Azurite 93

Chrysocolla 94

Turquoise 95

Aquamarine

STAR SIGN Pisces

PLANET Neptune

ELEMENT water

CHAKRA throat

· CRYSTAL TIPS ·

Carry aquamarine to help protect you from harm when
you are traveling, especially to foreign lands

◆

Put aquamarine on your desk when you are studying – its
tranquil energy enhances concentration

◆

Hold aquamarine when you have something you need to
say – it keeps you calm and helps you to communicate clearly

◆

Wear aquamarine to promote compassion

◆

Place aquamarine around you when meditating to help
you make contact with your inner self

◆

Like ocean waves lapping the shore, sea-colored aquamarine lets worries ebb

Sodalite

STAR SIGN Sagittarius

PLANET Jupiter

ELEMENT fire

CHAKRA brow

· CRYSTAL TIPS ·

Give each team member working on a project a sodalite
stone to bring forth ideas and creative expression

✦

Wear sodalite to lift your self-esteem and feel good
about yourself

✦

Sit quietly with sodalite if you feel confused so that your
mind can settle

✦

Give sodalite to your partner if he or she has difficulty
expressing feelings

✦

Keep sodalite near your bed if you work shifts, as
it helps to balance your sleep patterns

✦

Courageous sodalite chases away fears

Cavansite

STAR SIGN Aquarius

PLANET Uranus

ELEMENT air

CHAKRA brow

• CRYSTAL TIPS •

Place cavansite around you to give a 'feel-good' factor
to all that you do

✦

Put cavansite on your desk or in your workplace
to bring forth new ideas

✦

Position cavansite near you if you are a healer or work in the
caring professions to allow you to detach from clients' issues

✦

Keep cavansite near you to stimulate your psychic abilities

✦

Set cavansite next to your bed at night to help
you gain insight from your dreams

✦

Revitalizing cavansite encourages fresh insight

Lapis lazuli

STAR SIGN Sagittarius

PLANET Jupiter

ELEMENT fire

CHAKRA brow

· CRYSTAL TIPS ·

Carry lapis lazuli to enhance your natural abilities

✦

Put lapis lazuli in your bathroom to promote relaxation

✦

Give lapis lazuli to your partner to cement your relationship

✦

Lift your spirits with the energy of lapis lazuli – a 'feel-better'
stone to bring you out of depression

✦

Keep lapis lazuli around your home and office to
help you organize your life more efficiently

✦

Place lapis lazuli under your pillow to relieve insomnia

✦

Wisdom-enhancing lapis lazuli brings wonderment

Kyanite

STAR SIGN Libra

PLANET Venus

ELEMENT air

CHAKRA throat

· CRYSTAL TIPS ·

Place kyanite on your throat chakra if you are a singer
and your voice will benefit from its power

◆

Focus your mind on a kyanite crystal if you have difficulty
meditating to help you get started

◆

Wear kyanite to promote perseverance and mental stamina

◆

Place kyanite under your pillow to enhance dream recall
and interpretation

◆

Put kyanite around your home and workplace to help
you stay true to your purpose

◆

Carry kyanite to facilitate chakra alignment in
your energy body

◆

Kyanite's blue blades, like spiritual swords, help cut a path through life

Sapphire

STAR SIGN Virgo

PLANET Mercury

ELEMENT earth

CHAKRA brow

· CRYSTAL TIPS ·

Carry sapphire to help you fulfill your ambitions,
dreams and goals

✦

Wear sapphire to bring you intuition and wisdom

✦

Keep sapphire with you to promote your spiritual connection
and allow you to see the beauty in everything

✦

Meditate with sapphire to enhance contact
with your spirit guides

✦

Focus on an issue and hold sapphire to help you
see another's viewpoint

✦

Hold sapphire to swollen glands for relief

✦

Beautiful blue sapphire brings insight and happiness

Celestite

STAR SIGN Gemini

PLANET Mercury

ELEMENT air

CHAKRA brow

· **CRYSTAL TIPS** ·

Put celestite next to your bed to promote dreaming, chase
away nightmares and help with dream recall

◆

Place celestite near you to enhance your creative expression

◆

Keep celestite around you to help detox your mind of stress,
worries or despair

◆

Meditate with celestite to bring you closer to the
realms of the angels

◆

Carry celestite to balance your male and female
energies, helping you to achieve success in
all areas of your life

◆

Peaceful blue celestite promotes natural abilities

Azurite

STAR SIGN Sagittarius

PLANET Jupiter

ELEMENT fire

CHAKRA throat

· CRYSTAL TIPS ·

Keep azurite with you when you are in need of divine
guidance – it is known as the 'stone of heaven'

◆

Hold azurite to boost your clairvoyant abilities

◆

Position azurite near you if you are a healer to benefit
from the empathy it brings

◆

Carry or wear azurite to ease aching bones

◆

Hold azurite to assist you when you need to express
your deepest thoughts or feelings

◆

Place azurite in your workplace to help
stimulate creativity

◆

*Azurite helps you to see into life's mysteries and
increase spiritual attunement*

Chrysocolla

STAR SIGN Taurus

PLANET Venus

ELEMENT earth

CHAKRA heart

· CRYSTAL TIPS ·

Keep chrysocolla with you when you are
pregnant; its soothing energy is good for both you
and your unborn child

◆

Put chrysocolla in your garden to help balance the
Earth's natural energy

◆

Give yourself a boost of sexuality and revitalize your relationship
by placing chrysocolla around your bedroom

◆

Wear or carry chrysocolla to ease the symptoms of
premenstrual syndrome

◆

Give chrysocolla to friends whenever you feel
discretion is needed

◆

"Feel-better' chrysocolla helps to release tension

Turquoise

STAR SIGN Sagittarius

PLANET Jupiter

ELEMENT fire

CHAKRA throat

· CRYSTAL TIPS ·

Wear turquoise to protect you while traveling
and keep you safe from accidents

◆

Place turquoise in your home and car to keep
them safe and secure

◆

Hold turquoise to enhance communication and
creative expression

◆

Meditate with turquoise to help you bring your spiritual
experiences back into the physical world

◆

Carry turquoise if you feel unwell, as it
will ease most conditions

◆

Give turquoise to promote friendship,
love and romance

◆

Turquoise allows you to see the beauty in everything

Violet

Purple fluorite 98

Spirit quartz 99

Charoite 100

Ametrine 101

Lepidolite 102

Sugilite 103

Amethyst 104

Energizing violet crystals boost spiritual awareness

Purple fluorite

STAR SIGN Pisces

PLANET Neptune

ELEMENT water

CHAKRA crown

· CRYSTAL TIPS ·

Wear purple fluorite or keep it with you when learning new lessons to help you concentrate

✦

Hold purple fluorite for eloquence if you get stuck for words

✦

Place purple fluorite in a stressful workplace to assist your mental abilities

✦

Hold purple fluorite and focus on any issues troubling you – especially if you have been emotionally or physically unwell for some time and nothing seems to be helping

Soothing purple fluorite enhances understanding of dis-ease on a deep spiritual level

Spirit quartz

STAR SIGN Aquarius

PLANET Uranus

ELEMENT air

CHAKRA crown

· CRYSTAL TIPS ·

Keep spirit quartz with you to promote team building for sports
or in the workplace

✦

Place spirit quartz next to your bed to enhance dreams

✦

Hold spirit quartz to release emotion
and lift your energy, and for comfort
if you feel lonely

✦

Meditate with spirit quartz to access
your inner self and your past lives

✦

Work with spirit quartz to improve
your extrasensory perception

✦

Stimulating spirit quartz gives a sense of belonging

Charoite

STAR SIGN Sagittarius

PLANET Jupiter

ELEMENT fire

CHAKRA crown

· CRYSTAL TIPS ·

Wear charoite to slow down
and experience living in the moment

✦

Keep charoite with you to allow you to let go
of old relationships

✦

Carry charoite to help you see opportunities and move forward

✦

Leave charoite around you to make it easier
to focus your mind and meditate

✦

Place charoite near you at home and at work
to increase your intuition

✦

Hold charoite to increase your attention span

✦

*Motivating charoite brings
spiritual experiences into daily life*

Ametrine

STAR SIGN Libra

PLANET Venus

ELEMENT air

CHAKRA crown

· CRYSTAL TIPS ·

Keep ametrine around your workplace to bring inspiration and creativity

◆

Carry ametrine to help you overcome obstructions, prejudice and ignorance

◆

Leave ametrine where you meditate to speed the process of
stilling the mind

◆

Lie down and place ametrine on your solar plexus to
help remove emotional blockages

◆

Hold ametrine when you need to release tension

◆

Place ametrine around your home to bring peace and tranquility

◆

*Calming ametrine promotes
spiritual understanding*

Lepidolite

STAR SIGN Libra

PLANET Venus

ELEMENT air

CHAKRA heart

· CRYSTAL TIPS ·

Keep lepidolite near you while you study to boost concentration

◆

Place lepidolite in your living room to create a calm atmosphere

◆

Wear lepidolite to relieve stress-related conditions

◆

Carry lepidolite to release unkind feelings you may be holding

◆

Keep lepidolite near you to help free yourself from addictions

◆

Put lepidolite in the places you spend most time to help lift depression

◆

Reassuring lepidolite dispels negative thoughts

Sugilite

Empowering sugilite gives you the confidence to express yourself

STAR SIGN Virgo

PLANET Mercury

ELEMENT earth

CHAKRA crown

· CRYSTAL TIPS ·

Carry or wear sugilite to promote confidence and courage

✦

Place sugilite by your bed to ease worries and enhance mental rest

✦

Give sugilite as a sign of forgiveness

✦

Hold sugilite in your hand to draw the energy of physical discomfort from anywhere in your body

✦

Keep sugilite with you to allow yourself to express your eccentricities

✦

Put sugilite in the rooms of children who need to overcome learning difficulties

✦

Work with sugilite to help you find your life path

✦

Amethyst

STAR SIGNS Aquarius

PLANET Uranus

ELEMENT air

CHAKRA crown

· CRYSTAL TIPS ·

Wear amethyst to enhance your aura and boost your self-esteem

✦

Place amethyst throughout your home to bring relaxation,
health and happiness

✦

Hold amethyst to your head to ease headaches and migraines

✦

Keep amethyst near you to stop feeling homesick

✦

Meditate while holding an amethyst crystal in each hand
to enhance the flow of chi through your body

✦

Place your other crystals on a bed of amethyst to
reinvigorate them

✦

Vibrant amethyst brings revitalizing spiritual connection

Rainbow

Opal 108

✦

Bornite/peacock ore 109

✦

Rainbow obsidian 110

✦

Labradorite 111

✦

Abalone shell 112

✦

Watermelon tourmaline 113

✦

Angel aura quartz 114

✦

Titanium quartz 115

Rainbow crystals attract variety and originality into your life

Opal

STAR SIGN Cancer

PLANET Moon

ELEMENT water

CHAKRA throat

· CRYSTAL TIPS ·

Rub opal to enhance your memory

✦

Place opal around you at work to promote creativity,
inspiration and imagination

✦

Carry blue opal when you want to feel invisible – it is known
as the 'stone of thieves'

✦

Put opal in your pocket when you want to lose your inhibitions

✦

Wear opal to increase your sexual attraction

✦

Keep opal with you to promote diversity, since
'variety is the spice of life'

✦

Opal endows mystery and charisma

Bornite/peacock ore

STAR SIGN Cancer

PLANET Moon

ELEMENT water

CHAKRA all chakras

· **CRYSTAL TIPS** ·

Carry bornite to overcome self-imposed blocks and
move past their limitations

◆

Keep bornite around you to boost your physical energy

◆

Place bornite in your home to attract happiness into your life

◆

Meditate with bornite to help bring you into the present moment

◆

Allow the energy of bornite to soothe grief

◆

Put bornite under your pillow to promote equilibrium
between the left and right sides of your brain for a
balanced view of life

◆

Bornite speeds karmic healing

Rainbow obsidian

STAR SIGN Libra

PLANET Venus

ELEMENT air

CHAKRA base

· CRYSTAL TIPS ·

Wear rainbow obsidian to bring out your personal charisma

◆

Look into rainbow obsidian to see the future

◆

Place rainbow obsidian in your home to welcome happiness

◆

Meditate with rainbow obsidian to experience your inner self

◆

Carry rainbow obsidian when outdoors to enhance your
appreciation of nature

◆

Hold rainbow obsidian to release stress

◆

Life-enhancing rainbow obsidian attracts joy
and releases sadness

Labradorite

STAR SIGN Scorpio

PLANET Pluto

ELEMENT water

CHAKRA crown

· CRYSTAL TIPS ·

Wear labradorite to stabilize your aura and enhance the flow of energy
between your aura and chakras, boosting health and vitality

✦

Keep labradorite near you to increase your intuition and originality

✦

Tap labradorite gently on warts to encourage them to disappear

✦

Position labradorite in your workplace to let you see many
possibilities at once

✦

Put labradorite under your pillow and your mind will be sharper
the next day

✦

Carry labradorite to make magic happen
around you

✦

Magical labradorite inspires mental agility and intuitive powers

Abalone shell

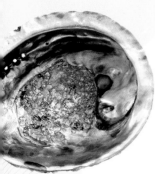

STAR SIGN Cancer

PLANET Moon

ELEMENT water

CHAKRA throat

· **CRYSTAL TIPS** ·

Wear abalone shell to let your femininity shine

✦

Place abalone shell in your bathroom to help you relax

✦

Hold abalone shell in a quiet place to help you release emotions

✦

Put abalone shell in your workplace to help relieve tension

✦

Carry abalone shell to allow you to see the beauty in the
world around you

✦

Wear or carry abalone shell when you need more power for
a special situation

✦

Tune into the wisdom of your ancestors with abalone shells from the depths of the sea

Watermelon tourmaline

STAR SIGN Virgo

PLANET Mercury

ELEMENT earth

CHAKRA heart

· CRYSTAL TIPS ·

Wear watermelon tourmaline to enhance discretion

✦

Carry watermelon tourmaline to help you see the funny side
of any situation

✦

Place watermelon tourmaline around your home to encourage humor

✦

Hold watermelon tourmaline to reduce nervousness

✦

Meditate with watermelon tourmaline to connect with your higher self

✦

Give watermelon tourmaline as a gift to promote love

✦

Keep reverse watermelon tourmaline near you if
you are thinking of traveling to help you set
your plans in motion

✦

Colorful watermelon tourmaline promotes a fun-filled life

Angel aura quartz

STAR SIGN all star signs

PLANET all planets

ELEMENT all elements

CHAKRA all chakras

· CRYSTAL TIPS ·

Hold angel aura quartz when you need comfort, letting
its energies nurture you

✦

Place angel aura quartz in your home to bring you harmony,
love and peace

✦

Keep angel aura quartz near you if you work in the caring professions
to help you detach from your clients' emotions

✦

Meditate with angel aura quartz to receive guidance from your angels

✦

Put angel aura quartz next to your bed to
protect you while you sleep

✦

Angel aura quartz helps you contact your angels

Titanium quartz

STAR SIGN all star signs

PLANET all planets

ELEMENT all elements

CHAKRA all chakras

· CRYSTAL TIPS ·

Carry titanium quartz to help you make a career decision

◆

Keep titanium quartz at work to allow you to see another's point of view

◆

Place titanium quartz around your home to keep illness at bay

◆

Encircle yourself with titanium quartz to promote a meditative experience

◆

Wear titanium quartz when you feel 'all over the place' to center
yourself and lift your emotions

◆

Hold titanium quartz to enhance
your ability to see auras

◆

Titanium quartz gives you that 'feel-good' factor

Multicolored crystals bring a multitude of benefits

Multicolored

Agate 118

Jasper 119

Onyx 120

Chalcedony 121

Tourmaline 122

Fluorite 123

Rhyolite 124

Calcite 125

Agate

STAR SIGN Gemini

PLANET Mercury

ELEMENT air

CHAKRA heart

· CRYSTAL TIPS ·

Give agate to your partner to promote faithfulness
in your relationship

◆

Put agate around your bed to balance your sexual energy

◆

Carry agate to ease an upset stomach

◆

Keep agate near you to bring you emotional security

◆

Wear agate to benefit from its protective 'force field',
which shields you from negativity

◆

Meditate with agate when you are unwell to help
make an accurate diagnosis

◆

Shielding agate stops harmful energies from penetrating your aura

jasper

STAR SIGN Leo

PLANET Sun

ELEMENT fire

CHAKRA base

· CRYSTAL TIPS ·

Wear jasper to balance your aura

✦

Put jasper next to your bed for comfort if you feel lonely

✦

Hold jasper to improve your accuracy when dowsing

✦

Carry jasper to prevent illness

✦

Place jasper around your home to reduce arguments

✦

Balancing jasper helps you achieve your goals

Onyx

STAR SIGN Leo

PLANET Sun

ELEMENT fire

CHAKRA base

· CRYSTAL TIPS ·

Put onyx in your home to bring luck and happiness

♦

Hold onyx to help you to make decisions

♦

Place onyx in a bowl of warm water to soothe aching feet
at the end of a tiring day

♦

Keep onyx at your workplace to take charge of situations

♦

Meditate with onyx to connect to your roots and your
spiritual path

♦

Lucky onyx helps you to take charge of your life

Chalcedony

STAR SIGN Cancer

PLANET Moon

ELEMENT water

CHAKRA throat

· CRYSTAL TIPS ·

Carry chalcedony to help you lose weight

◆

Place chalcedony in your home to promote a balance
between male and female energies for a calm ambience

◆

Hold chalcedony to improve your telepathic link if you feel
connected to another person (who should hold it, too)

◆

Put chalcedony under your pillow to release you gently
from the trauma of past experiences

◆

Hold chalcedony to relieve stress

◆

Wear chalcedony to stop you worrying excessively

◆

Nurturing chalcedony promotes peace and understanding

Tourmaline

STAR SIGN Libra

PLANET Venus

ELEMENT air

CHAKRA all

· CRYSTAL TIPS ·

Wear tourmaline, and place it at home and
in your car, to safeguard you from harm

Carry tourmaline to help you face new challenges

Place tourmaline in your workplace for group bonding

Keep tourmaline near you if you are a healer to boost
your abilities

Keep tourmaline with you to increase self-confidence

Put tourmaline next to your bed to ease a troubled
mind and promote restful sleep

Hold tourmaline to alleviate fear

Morale-boosting tourmaline brings courage and purpose

Fluorite

STAR SIGN Pisces

PLANET Neptune

ELEMENT water

CHAKRA brow

· CRYSTAL TIPS ·

Put fluorite on your desk to focus your mind

✦

Give a gift of fluorite to bond a relationship

✦

Place fluorite in children's bedrooms to reduce overexcitability at night

✦

Carry fluorite to help overcome eating disorders

✦

Place fluorite on your desk to reduce the tiring effect of computer screens

✦

Leave fluorite anywhere you need to create order from chaos

✦

Wear fluorite to help your body to detox

✦

Mind-stilling fluorite is conducive to meditation

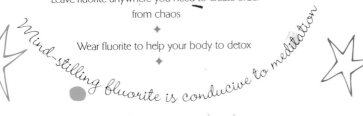

Rhyolite

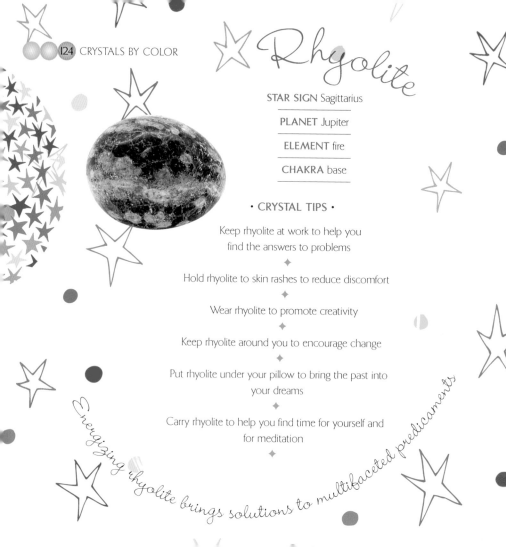

STAR SIGN Sagittarius

PLANET Jupiter

ELEMENT fire

CHAKRA base

· CRYSTAL TIPS ·

Keep rhyolite at work to help you
find the answers to problems

✦

Hold rhyolite to skin rashes to reduce discomfort

✦

Wear rhyolite to promote creativity

✦

Keep rhyolite around you to encourage change

✦

Put rhyolite under your pillow to bring the past into
your dreams

✦

Carry rhyolite to help you find time for yourself and
for meditation

✦

Energizing rhyolite brings solutions to multifaceted predicaments

Calcite

STAR SIGN Cancer

PLANET Moon

ELEMENT water

CHAKRA various depending on variety

· CRYSTAL TIPS ·

Put calcite in the rooms of growing children to promote healthy bones

✦

Hold calcite to relieve stress and bring calm

✦

Place calcite on your desk when studying or teaching to aid the calm, clear flow of information

✦

Keep calcite at work to help you see the bigger picture

✦

Wear calcite to temper overenthusiasm

✦

'Feel-better' calcite frees you from fear

White and clear crystals stimulate insight and positive energy

White and Clear

Quartz 128

❖

Apophyllite 129

❖

Diamond 130

❖

Herkimer diamond 131

❖

Tibetan quartz 132

❖

Phantom quartz 133

❖

Selenite 134

❖

Moonstone 135

❖

Quartz

STAR SIGN all star signs

PLANET all planets

ELEMENT all elements

CHAKRA all chakras

Bring light into your life with quartz crystal

· CRYSTAL TIPS ·

Hold quartz to any sore areas of your body to ease pain
– it is the ultimate healing crystal

◆

Put quartz crystals on your desk to focus energy and inspiration
toward your work

◆

Place a quartz crystal cluster in your living room to bring light
and happiness into your home

◆

Leave a quartz crystal cluster next to your bed to reenergize you
while you sleep

◆

Wear quartz to surround yourself with healing energy

◆

Meditate with quartz to focus
your mind

◆

Apophyllite

STAR SIGN Gemini

PLANET Mercury

ELEMENT air

CHAKRA crown

· CRYSTAL TIPS ·

Place apophyllite in your kitchen to help keep food fresh

✦

Meditate with apophyllite to keep the inner calm of the meditative
state after finishing your practice

✦

Look into an apophyllite crystal to see the future

✦

Place pyramidal apophyllite crystals around your bed to rejuvenate
you as you sleep

✦

Wear apophyllite to promote truth in yourself and others
you come into contact with

✦

Hold apophyllite when you need
a boost of brain power

✦

Energizing apophyllite revitalizes the soul

Diamond

STAR SIGN Aries

PLANET Sun

ELEMENT fire

CHAKRA all chakras

· CRYSTAL TIPS ·

Give diamond to express love

◆

Carry diamond to encourage new beginnings and projects

◆

Place diamond under your pillow to increase your spiritual awareness

◆

Put a diamond in your purse or wallet to bring abundance and wealth

◆

Meditate with diamond to gain self-acceptance

◆

Keep diamond with you to aid detox on all levels: mental,
spiritual and physical

◆

Leave diamond in your home to bring in
positive energy that will benefit body
and spirit

◆

Powerful, life-enhancing diamond promotes bravery and courage

Herkimer diamond

STAR SIGN Sagittarius

PLANET Jupiter

ELEMENT fire

CHAKRA crown

· CRYSTAL TIPS ·

Hold Herkimer diamond when you need to remember
something from the past

✦

Put Herkimer diamond under your pillow to promote relaxation
and aid a restful night's sleep

✦

Wear Herkimer diamond to bring spontaneity into your life

✦

Meditate with Herkimer diamond to increase your psychic abilities

✦

Carry Herkimer diamond to lessen stress

✦

Work with the supportive energies of Herkimer
diamond in ceremonies or rituals

✦

Brilliant Herkimer diamond clears troubles from the mind

Tibetan quartz

STAR SIGN all star signs

PLANET all planets

ELEMENT all elements

CHAKRA all chakras

· CRYSTAL TIPS ·

Hold Tibetan quartz while you are talking to help you get to the point
if you have a tendency to rattle on

◆

Meditate with Tibetan quartz to bring you a deeper spiritual
connection

◆

Wear Tibetan quartz to stimulate your chi, helping you to feel great

◆

Place Tibetan quartz by your bed to keep negative emotions
at bay

◆

Carry Tibetan quartz to promote weight loss

◆

Cleansing Tibetan quartz gives clarity

Phantom quartz

STAR SIGN all star signs

PLANET all planets

ELEMENT all elements

CHAKRA crown

• CRYSTAL TIPS •

Keep phantom quartz near you to help you see the hidden meanings behind what is happening in your life

✦

Meditate with phantom quartz to find your inner self

✦

Carry phantom quartz to dispel negative emotions

✦

Put phantom quartz in your work area to see the truth in situations around you

✦

Work with phantom quartz to contact the spirit world

✦

Place phantom quartz by your telephone to give you insight as to what the caller really means by their words

✦

Phantom quartz opens channels to hidden truths and the inner self

Selenite

Crystals of Selene, Goddess of the Moon

STAR SIGN Taurus

PLANET Venus

ELEMENT earth

CHAKRA crown

· CRYSTAL TIPS ·

Work with the lunar energy of selenite to
encourage a positive flow of events in your life

✦

Leave selenite in your bedroom to increase your sex drive
– it is linked to Venus and stimulates female energy

✦

Keep selenite with you to slow the onset of baldness

✦

Put selenite in your bathroom to reduce the aging of your skin

✦

Place selenite in your home to bring longevity

✦

Moonstone

STAR SIGN Cancer

PLANET Moon

ELEMENT water

CHAKRA sacral

· CRYSTAL TIPS ·

Carry moonstone to relieve the symptoms of premenstrual syndrome

✦

Wear moonstone to prevent you from repeating negative patterns

✦

Hold moonstone to soothe your emotions

✦

Lie down and place moonstone on your sacral chakra
to release energy blocks

✦

Give moonstone to promote caring in relationships

✦

Place moonstone around you to bring peace of mind

✦

Keep moonstone in your bathroom to promote
a youthful appearance

✦

Soothing moonstone inspires fresh insight

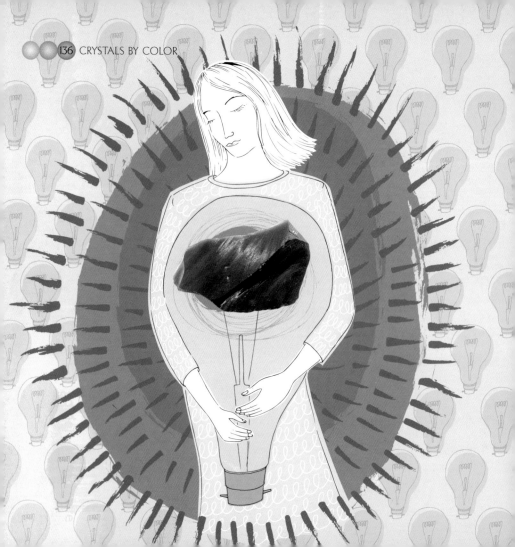

Black and Gray

Jet 138

Merlinite 139

Tektite 140

Obsidian 141

Hematite 142

Silver 143

Pyrite 144

Stibnite 145

Jet

STAR SIGN Capricorn

PLANET Saturn

ELEMENT earth

CHAKRA base

· CRYSTAL TIPS ·

Keep jet in your bedroom to increase sexual energy

✦

Carry or wear jet to relieve the symptoms of migraine headaches

✦

Leave a piece of jet by your bank statements to attract money to your account

✦

Wear jet to protect you from illness

✦

Carry jet to help alleviate depression and anxiety

✦

Place jet in your home to bring in grounded energy for a feeling of stability

✦

Stabilizing jet dispels fear

Merlinite

STAR SIGN Pisces

PLANET Neptune

ELEMENT water

CHAKRA brow

· CRYSTAL TIPS ·

Keep merlinite handy if you are negotiating an agreement
to allow you to see both sides of a debate

◆

Carry merlinite to promote optimism and help you seize the moment

◆

Leave merlinite in your special space to enhance your psychic abilities

◆

Wear merlinite to let magic happen around you

◆

Keep merlinite in your car or on your bicycle to boost
your survival instincts

◆

Place merlinite in your home to create a calm
and magical atmosphere

◆

Merlinite, the crystal magician, brings hope and courage

Tektite

STAR SIGN Aries

PLANET Mars

ELEMENT fire

CHAKRA crown

· **CRYSTAL TIPS** ·

Hold tektite if you are an astrologer for a psychic connection
to the stars and planets

◆

Carry tektite to improve your reasoning ability

◆

For a wonderful spiritual experience, meditate
with tektite (see pages 22–23)

◆

Place tektite around your home to balance male and female
energies for a revitalizing atmosphere

◆

Work with tektite to
contact other worlds

◆

Inspirational tektite links astrologers to the stars

Obsidian

STAR SIGN Sagittarius

PLANET Jupiter

ELEMENT fire

CHAKRA base

• CRYSTAL TIPS •

Look into obsidian to see your true self and your future

✦

Give obsidian – the mirror of the soul – as a symbol of wisdom

✦

Wear obsidian for protection from accidents and to
dispel unkind thoughts

✦

Keep obsidian with you to promote understanding when learning
new skills and concepts

✦

Meditate with obsidian to allow its male energy to stimulate
your dynamic masculine side

✦

Place obsidian by your bed to help release
trapped tears from past events

✦

Grounding obsidian brings you down to earth

Hematite

STAR SIGN Aries

PLANET Mars

ELEMENT fire

CHAKRA base

· CRYSTAL TIPS ·

Wear hematite to enhance your personal magnetism

✦

Give hematite as a gift to those who need strength to cope
with a situation

✦

Place hematite on your desk to stimulate your mathematical
abilities if you work with numbers

✦

Carry hematite when flying to alleviate the symptoms of jet lag

✦

Wear or carry hematite to enhance mental processes,
including memory and clarity of thought

✦

Hold hematite to ground you when
you feel spaced out

Hematite helps you keep your feet on the ground

Silver

STAR SIGN Cancer

PLANET Moon

ELEMENT water

CHAKRA crown

· CRYSTAL TIPS ·

Wear silver to improve your eloquence when you are in company or making a speech

Hold silver to amplify the healing energy of kind thoughts sent to friends in need

◆

Place your other crystals near silver during a full or new Moon to energize them

◆

Leave silver around your home to help you pass through transitions in the different stages of life, and to bring emotional balance

◆

Keep silver with you to promote mental health and emotional healing

◆

Silver gives every cloud a silver lining

Pyrite

STAR SIGN Leo

PLANET Sun

ELEMENT fire

CHAKRA solar plexus

· CRYSTAL TIPS ·

Place pyrite on each window sill to keep the sound of noisy neighbors at bay

◆

Put pyrite under your pillow to prevent you from snoring

◆

Hold pyrite when you need a reviving surge of energy

◆

Keep pyrite around you if you are a leader to benefit from its confidence-boosting powers

◆

Wear pyrite to protect you from harm

◆

Leave pyrite in your home to remove negativity and replace it with fresh, positive energy

◆

Known as 'fool's gold', pyrite projects power

Stibnite

STAR SIGN Scorpio

PLANET Pluto

ELEMENT water

CHAKRA crown

· CRYSTAL TIPS ·

Give stibnite as a gift to promote loyalty

◆

Work with stibnite to bring you speed and endurance

◆

Place stibnite around you to ease a relationship that has
become too clingy

◆

Hold stibnite to connect you to your spirit and totem animals

◆

Keep stibnite near you to guide you in decision-making

◆

Stibnite, the 'pathfinder' of crystals, shows you the way

Brown crystals stabilize emotions and boost stamina

Brown

Muscovite 148

Rutile 149

Aragonite 150

Lingham 151

Fulgurite 152

Chiastolite 153

Smoky quartz 154

Meteorite 155

Muscovite

STAR SIGN Aquarius

PLANET Uranus

ELEMENT air

CHAKRA heart

· CRYSTAL TIPS ·

Place muscovite on your desk to speed thoughts and problem solving

✦

Keep muscovite around you to safeguard yourself and those you are in contact with from negative energies and emotions

✦

Put muscovite by your bed to relieve insomnia

✦

Carry muscovite to give you confidence if you are feeling insecure

✦

Set muscovite in your new home to release energies trapped from the previous occupants

✦

Hold muscovite to listen to your intuition

✦

Calming muscovite brings clear insights

Rutile

STAR SIGN Gemini

PLANET Mercury

ELEMENT air

CHAKRA brow

· CRYSTAL TIPS ·

Keep rutile near you when you are feeling unwell to help treat the
cause of dis-ease

◆

Meditate with rutile, also known as angel hair, to benefit from the protective
energies of angels

◆

Place rutile near your bed to boost your aura while you sleep

◆

Work with rutile to gain insight into your sexuality

◆

Set rutile on your brow chakra to improve your state
of mind if you feel restless

◆

Heavenly rutile promotes harmony and a sense of peace

Aragonite

STAR SIGN Capricorn

PLANET Saturn

ELEMENT earth

CHAKRA crown

· CRYSTAL TIPS ·

Hold aragonite when you find yourself stuck for an answer, and the answer will suddenly become obvious

◆

Keep aragonite near you at work to encourage patience, practicality and reliability

◆

Hold aragonite to areas of general aches and pains for relief

◆

Place aragonite near your bed to promote a healthy glow when you wake

◆

Put aragonite against affected areas to heal stress-related skin conditions such as eczema and psoriasis

◆

Reviving aragonite stills the mind and boosts health

Lingham

STAR SIGN Scorpio

PLANET Pluto

ELEMENT water

CHAKRA all chakras

· CRYSTAL TIPS ·

Place lingham under your pillow to enhance fertility

Put lingham under your bed to ease back pain

Meditate with two lingham stones, one in each hand, for a spiritual
detox followed by a peak experience

Carry lingham to bolster your vigorous male side

Keep lingham with you to help you form links in your
mind between your physical world and
your spiritual path

Dynamic lingham brings spiritual understanding

Fulgurite

STAR SIGN Gemini

PLANET Mercury

ELEMENT air

CHAKRA brow

· CRYSTAL TIPS ·

Keep fulgurite near you to benefit from its energies – formed when lightning strikes the desert sands, it represents the fusion of heaven and earth that can bring paradise to its holder

✦

Carry fulgurite when speaking to ease channels of communication

✦

Keep fulgurite near you to boost concentration

✦

Hold fulgurite when dowsing for improved accuracy

✦

Meditate with fulgurite to develop your psychic abilities

✦

Place fulgurite in your bedroom to bring a spark back into relationships

✦

Powerful fulgurite boosts your love life

Chiastolite

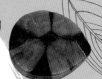

STAR SIGN Libra

PLANET Venus

ELEMENT air

CHAKRA sacral

• CRYSTAL TIPS •

The sign of the cross in the crystal is traditionally associated
with chiastolite's healing energies

✦

Take chiastolite to bed with you to help recovery from a fever

✦

Give chiastolite as a sign of devotion

✦

Keep chiastolite at work to assist with problem-solving and creativity

✦

Wear chiastolite when you need strength in difficult situations

✦

Carry chiastolite to bring good fortune – give
it a rub when you feel you need luck

✦

Chiastolite is healing and nurturing

Smoky quartz

STAR SIGN Capricorn

PLANET Saturn

ELEMENT earth

CHAKRA base

· CRYSTAL TIPS ·

Wear smoky quartz to dispel negative energy

◆

Put smoky quartz in your bedroom to boost sexuality

◆

Place smoky quartz by your bed to enhance dream interpretation

◆

Hold smoky quartz to increase the healing energy that flows
through your hands

◆

Keep smoky quartz near you at times of loss to ease grief

◆

Place smoky quartz in your living room to bring
calm and help you ground your energies and
relax at the end of the day

◆

Grounding smoky quartz encourages peace

Meteorite

STAR SIGN all star signs

PLANET all planets

ELEMENT all elements

CHAKRA crown

• CRYSTAL TIPS •

Give meteorite to rekindle bonds with distant friends and loved ones

♦

Hold meteorite to alleviate homesickness

♦

Place meteorite around you to relieve a feeling of melancholy

♦

Carry meteorite to boost your endurance

♦

Work with meteorite if you are emigrating
to ease the journey

♦

Hold meteorite in your hand to connect with
the universe

♦

Cosmic rocks are 4.5 billion years old

Resources

UK Resources

Cavern Crystals
www.crystalcavern.com

Crystals
Stores across southern
England and Wales
www.crystalshop.co.uk

Crystal Well-Being
+44 (0)1726 833936
www.crystalwellbeing.co.uk

Easy Crystals
+44 (0)7781 410223
www.easycrystals.co.uk

Earthlight Crystals
+44(0)1686 411139
www.earthlightcrystals.co.uk

Global Crystals
+44 (0)113 2461824
www.globalcrystals.com

Grailstones
www.grailstones.co.uk

Holistic Shop
+44 (0)1953 857260
www.holisticshop.co.uk

Patinkas
+44 (0)1730 239326
www.patinkas.co.uk

Shaman's Crystals
+44 (0)1234 360893
www.shamanscrystals.co.uk

Spirit Adventures
+44 (0)1843 836735
www.spiritadventures.co.uk

The Crystal Healer
www.thecrystalhealer.co.uk

The Crystal Shop
+44 (0)1334 479445
www.crystalshopscotland.com

US Resources

Best Crystals
503-285-4078
www.bestcrystals.com

Coleman's Crystal Mines and
Rock Shop
501-984-5328
www.jimcolemancrystals.com

Earth Gallery
415-302-0184
www.earthgallery.com

Earth-love Gallery
303-274-5088
3266 Youngsfield, Wheat Rodge,
CO 80033

Exquisite Crystals
360-573-6787
www.exquisitecrystals.com

Healing Crystals
703-828-4325
www.healingcrystals.com

Jeanne's Rock & Jewelry
713-664-2988
www.jeannesrockshop.com

Mineral Miners
877-464-6377
www.mineralminers.com

Peaceful Mind
www.peacefulmind.com

The Crystal Garden
561-369-2836
www.thecrystalgarden.com

The Crystal Room
530-918-9108
www.CrystalsMtShasta.com

Zedel International
www.zedel.com

Index of Crystals

abalone shell 112
agate 27, 118
amazonite 73
amber 11, 25, 59
amethyst 15, 17, 19, 27, 104
ametrine 101
angel aura quartz 114
apatite 54
apophyllite 129
aquamarine 27, 86
aragonite 25, 150
aventurine 65
azurite 93

bloodstone 11, 63
bornite 109

calcite 125
carnelian 19, 25, 27, 45
cavansite 88
celestite 92
chalcedony 121
charoite 100
chiastolite 153
chrysocolla 94
chrysoprase 11, 71
citrine 17, 19, 27, 53
copper 57
crocoite 25, 49

diamond 27, 130
dioptase 70

emerald 27, 69
erythrite 25, 78
eudialyte 83

falcon's eye 38
fluorite 123
fuchsite 25, 64
fulgurite 152

garnet 27, 35
gold 56
green calcite 68

halite 25, 44
hematite 25, 142
herkimer diamond 11, 131

imperial topaz 58

jade 25, 62
jasper 119
jet 138

kunzite 76
kyanite 27, 90

labradorite 111
lapis lazuli 19, 21, 89
lepidolite 102
lingham 151

malachite 19, 27, 66
merlinite 139

meteorite 9, 155
mookaite 37
moonstone 25, 27, 135
morganite 23, 82
muscovite 148

obsidian 141
onyx 120
opal 108
orange calcite 42

peacock ore 109
peridot 17, 27, 72
phantom quartz 133
pink opal 80
purple fluorite 98
pyrite 144

quartz 15, 17, 128

rainbow obsidian 110
red calcite 39
red jasper 19, 27, 33
rhodochrosite 77
rhodonite 79
rhyolite 124
rose quartz 17, 25, 27, 81
ruby 27, 36
rutile 149

sapphire 23, 27, 91
selenite 27, 134
silver 143

smoky quartz 154
sodalite 27, 87
spessartine 43
spinel 32
spirit quartz 99
stibnite 21, 145
sugilite 103
sunstone 47

tektite 9, 140
tibetan quartz 132
tiger's eye 52
titanium quartz 8, 115
tourmaline 122
turquoise 95

unakite 67

vanadinite 25, 48

watermelon tourmaline 113
wulfenite 46

yellow fluorite 55

zircon 27, 34

General Index

aches and pains 65, 81, 93, 128, 151
addictions 76, 102
allergic reaction 34
amethyst bed 15, 104
angels 92, 114, 148
anger 63, 69
anxiety 60, 68, 71, 121
arguments 119
asthma 48
awareness, heightened 46

back pain 151
baldness 134
base chakra 18, 19, 32, 33, 34, 37
beginnings, new 130
birthstones 26–7
black/gray crystals 136–145
blue crystals 21, 84–95
breath 15
breathing 22
brow chakra 18, 19
brown crystals 146–155

calming 57, 64, 73, 81, 125
career decisions 115
carrying crystals 20
centerpieces 8–9
ceremonies and rituals 131
chakras 18–19
Chaldeans 26
    planets and crystals 27
chaos, reducing 35, 123
children 39, 62, 70, 103, 123, 125
clarity 71, 87, 111, 115, 142

clear crystals 126–135
colds and flu 33, 45
colors 7
communication 78, 86, 95, 98, 132, 133, 143, 152
compassion 86
computer screens 123
concentration 86, 98, 100, 102, 152
confidence 37, 103, 122
courage 77, 103
creativity 49, 53, 54, 55, 73, 87, 88, 92
    musical 79
crown chakra 18, 19
crystals
    for chakras 19
    choosing 12–13
    cleansing 14–15
    defined 8–9
    how they work 10–11
    for space 17

decision-making 37, 120, 145
depression 34, 35, 66, 89, 102, 138
detachment 88, 114
dexterity 71
divine guidance 93
'divorce stone' (crocoite) 49
dowsing 119, 152
dreams 62, 66, 82, 88, 90, 92, 99, 124, 154

elixirs 24–5
emotional balance 43, 101, 109, 143

emotional energy 39, 72
emotional recovery 64, 66, 71, 77, 82, 141
energizing 32, 43, 45, 58, 65, 72, 109, 111, 128
exhaustion 48, 57
eyes 83

faithfulness 118
fear and panic 39, 47, 52, 68, 122
feet, aching 47, 120
femininity 76, 112, 134
fertility 38, 69, 151
fevers 153
focusing the mind 100, 101
forgiveness 103

geodes 15
gifts, crystals as 21
glands, swollen 91
green crystals 60–73
gray/black crystals 136–145
grief 67, 105, 109, 154

headaches and migraine 104, 138
healing powers 10–11, 18–19, 88, 93, 122, 128
health 54, 68, 69, 70, 115
heart chakra 18, 19, 35, 36
heart and circulation 70
homesickness 104, 155
humor 113

identifying crystals 7